The flute Book

Atarah Ben-Tovim

Illustrated by Cathy Brear

List of musical excerpts

6 (top) *Pavana*, anon; 7 (top) *Dance of the Blessed Spirits*, Gluck; (center) *Study*, Hotteterre; 9 (top) *Study*, Boehm; (center) *Le Merle Blanc*, Damaré; (bottom) *The Irish Washerwoman*, traditional; 12 (top) *Irish Jig*, traditional; 13 (top) *Tambourin*, Gossec; 14 (top) *Exercise*, Moyse; 15 (top) *Greensleeves*, traditional; 16 (top) *Eine Kleine Nachtmusik*, Mozart; (bottom) *Frère Jacques*, traditional round; 17 (top) *Concerto in G*, Mozart; (center) *Concerto in D*, Mozart; (bottom) *Suite in B minor, Badinerie*, J.S. Bach; 18 (top) *Sicilienne*, Fauré; 19 (top) *Flight of the Bumblebee*, Rimsky Korsakov; 20 (top) *Andante*, Mozart; 25 (top) *Il Était une Bergère*, anon; 27 (top) *Morceau de Concours*, Fauré; 34 (top) *Suite in A minor, Air Italien*, Telemann; 35 (top) *Variations on a Theme of Rossini*, Chopin; 36 & 37 (top) duet taken from *Trio Sonata*, Quantz; 38 (top) aria from *The Magic Flute*, Mozart; (center) *Sheherazade*, Ravel; (bottom) *Syrinx*, Debussy; 39 (center) *Krishna*, Roussel; (bottom) *I Heard a Piper Piping,* from *Six Irish Folk Songs*, Bax; 40 & 41 duet *O, Susannah*, traditional; 44 (top) *Rondo,* Mozart; 45 (top) *Sonata*, Poulenc.

Acknowledgments

Pictures

We are grateful to the following for permission to reproduce the pictures in this book.

AKG Photos: 27 (SMPK, Nationalgalerie, Berlin).
Bridgeman Art Library: **cover** (Museo Correr, Venice); 40 (Hermitage, St Petersburg).
By courtesy of *The British Library*: 7 (MSS Add. 19352).
Escorial, Madrid: 36.
Marc Grauwels: 27.
Trevor James: 13.
Paul Lane: 27 (donation to C.H.E.O.)
Hamish Mitchell: 9; 41; 42; 44.
Musée d'Orsay, Paris: 26.
Pan Magazine, Journal of the British Flute Society: 10 (Douglas Bardwell).
Katie Vandyck: 8; 23.
Trevor Wye: 9.
Zefa Pictures: 41.

The photographs of the author's own collection were taken by *Douglas Boyd*. Thanks also to Julie Wright, Trevor Wye, and Albert Cooper, and to the children who appear in the photographs.

The author and publishers have made every effort to trace the owners of copyright material. Any queries should be addressed to the publishers.

Cover: Detail from **The Music Party** by Pieter Van Aelst (1502 - 50), Museo Correr, Venice.

The Flute Book

Contents

How old is the flute?

Nobody knows when the first flute was made, but excavations of Stone Age caves in France have revealed small flutes carved out of pierced bones by Ice Age hunters more than 20,000 years ago! They were probably for playing bird-calls, used to entice birds within range of the hunters' weapons.

Bone flute

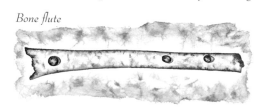

Han Hsiang-Tzu

Early flutes were end-blown, like a modern descant recorder. In some parts of the world primitive flutes of this variety are played by positioning the open end of the flute beneath one nostril and blowing hard! The method of holding the flute sideways and blowing across the open hole to make a more powerful sound dates back at least 3,000 years, as proven by silk scroll pictures and poems from China. Han Hsiang-Tzu, one of the eight Taoist immortals, is always depicted playing such a flute.

Krishna

Ancient Egyptian wall-paintings show many transverse flutes (held sideways). The god Osiris was credited with inventing several kinds of flutes to be played during religious ceremonies, but we don't know what they sounded like. The Ancient Greeks preferred the double-reed flute called the aulos, which is still played in Arab countries. When you have heard one, you will understand why "pandemonium" was the word for the madness caused by Pan playing this kind of flute! If his music was devilish, in India the flute was considered divine: The god Krishna played a transverse flute to call his followers to salvation. 2,000 years ago the Romans had flutes made of bronze, possibly with wooden mouthpieces. It is frustrating that we do not really know much about the music they played.

6

Medieval manuscript illustration of David with his sheep

Many medieval frescoes and manuscript illustrations show shepherds playing simple, keyless, transverse flutes to their flocks, but the earliest transverse flute of which we know the shape, the size and the music (see top of page 6) is the Renaissance flute. A simple one-piece tube of boxwood or ivory, it had six finger-holes and sounded a primary scale of D major. Flutes like this existed in four sizes: descant, alto, tenor, and bass. The D major flute was also known as the fife (from the German for "pipe") and was used for military music, usually with a drum.

Renaissance flute

We owe the basic idea of our modern flute to a Frenchman named Jacques-Martin Hotteterre. In 1707, he invented the Baroque flute by adding a seventh hole for D sharp, plus a key by which to open and close it, using the little finger. (The range was described as "two octaves and some notes." Today we have a range of three octaves and some notes.) He was the first person to make a flute that separated into the three parts we know today: the head-joint, the body with its finger-holes, and the foot-joint. This makes it possible to tune the flute to other instruments for ensemble playing. Hotteterre also wrote music for the flute, like this:

Hotteterre flute

After Hotteterre had the basic idea, other players and inventors added additional keys, not to extend the range of the flute but to simplify and tune the very complicated cross-fingerings necessary to obtain some of the notes. Christoph Gluck composed *The Dance of the Blessed Spirits* in 1760 (see top of page). Mozart also wrote his flute concertos for this kind of hybrid flute.

7

The flute you play

From 1707 to 1832 flutes became technically more complicated as different inventors added extra keys, pillars, plates, tenons, and sockets until hardly any two flutes looked alike or were played in the same way. People even experimented with glass and porcelain flutes – which worked fine until somebody dropped them!

In 1832 Theobald Boehm, a flutist from Munich who was also a metal-worker, thought this was crazy and sat down to redesign the flute. At first he had twelve holes (one for each semitone of the chromatic scale). Because these holes had to be in certain places for technical reasons, some of them did not lie under the player's fingers.

Old system

New system

In any case, no one has twelve fingers with which to stop the holes, so Boehm invented a system of rods and keys that enabled the player to sound all the notes without changing the position of the fingers. To show what a genius he was, he wrote many studies so difficult that only an octopus could have played them on earlier flutes (see top of page 9)! His experiments lasted fifteen years. By 1847 he had produced a "Patent Flute" with sixteen holes that was the model of all the orchestral flutes we play today. Whether your flute is made of wood, nickel, silver, or gold, it is still a Boehm-system flute. Now every flute player has a whole new world of possibilities to explore and enjoy with all the digital and other electronic devices available.

Theobald Boehm

The transverse flute family

There are several other flutes of different sizes. The bigger they are, the lower they sound. All are played with the same fingering. Once you have learned one, you can easily play any of the others. The baby of the family is the **piccolo**. About 1 foot (30.5 cm) long, or less than half the length of a flute, it sounds a whole octave higher. Beware! Small does not mean easier to play; it is more difficult to make a nice sound and be in tune on the piccolo than on the flute.

Trevor Wye with a range of flutes

Damaré's Le Merle Blanc *for piccolo*

Bigger (and five semi-tones lower) than the concert flute is the **alto** flute, which is often heard in jazz music, like this improvisation:

Jazz improvisation

Alto flute

Some alto flutes have curved head-joints to make them more comfortable to play. And so do some of the biggest and lowest flutes of all: the **bass** flutes.

First cousins with the same fingering are the **G treble** instrument (found in Irish flute bands), the **E♭** flute in American wind bands, and the **flute d'amour**, which is used for old music.

Lower than even the bass flute is the **contrabass** and lower still is the **subcontrabass**, which is twelve feet long and sounds three octaves below the flute! Distant cousins are **fifes** (in military bands), the **Baroque** flutes used to play Early Music, and traditional or **folk** flutes (see music below) from many countries.

9

Making a flute

Flute makers serve a five-year apprenticeship learning their craft, which includes operating the precision machines that cut, draw, shape, and solder the pieces.

The most difficult part to get right is the one that looks simplest: If the **head-joint** is wrong, the flute will never sound good. This piece of tube is slightly conical (cone shaped). The **lip plate** is shaped and the embouchure hole cut by hand to the right size with the blowing edge at the correct angle for your breath to vibrate the column of air in the body of the flute.

tenon for body

head-joint

blowing edge

left-hand key

embouchure hole

direction of air stream

body

crown

lip-plate

socket for head-joint

pillar

Flute-maker Albert Cooper at work.

The top end is stopped by a **crown** which, by means of a screw, controls the position of a cork inside the tube. Moving this cork minutely changes the length of the column of air in the flute – and therefore the relative pitch of every note played. Professional flutists are always looking for the perfect head-joint. Some travel across the world to buy one specially made for them by makers like Jack Frazer in Ireland, Muramatsu in Japan, Albert Cooper in England, Faulisi in France, Eva Kingma in Holland, and all the fine flute makers in the USA.

The rest of the flute is made from two pieces of cylindrical tubing with a constant diameter (³/₄ in. or 19mm). Each piece has a socket soldered on one end, into which the tenon of the next piece fits. A narrower tube is cut into tiny pieces that are drawn and soldered into place to make the **tone holes**. When all this has been done very precisely, the flute maker has to fit by hand all the **pillars, rods, keys, rollers, springs** – more than 150 different bits and pieces. No wonder flutes cost quite a lot of money to buy! The awful thing is that one little screw that is too tight or too slack can ruin a flute…, which is why it is always worth buying a good one.

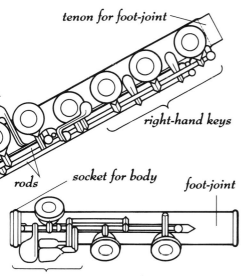

tenon for foot-joint

right-hand keys

rods

socket for body

foot-joint

**right-hand little finger keys
(for lowest notes)**

It is a good idea to know the names of the most important parts. Get someone to test you.

Famous makers

How many of these famous flute makers' names do you know?
Abell, Altus, Armstrong, Bigio, Boosey and Hawkes, Buffet-Crampon, Cooper, Earlham, Gemeinhardt, Hammig, Haynes, Trevor James, Jupiter, Louis Lot, John Lunn, Mateki, McLauchlan, Miyazawa, Moenig, Muramatsu, Natsuki, Oxley, Oston Brannen Brothers, Pearl, Powell, Rudall Carte, Sankyo, Selmer, Yamaha.

Wordsearch

*Can you find the names of
12 flute makers?*
(Answers on page 44)

C	A	R	T	E	T	T	R	E	V
S	O	L	E	G	E	R	R	O	K
A	L	P	L	J	F	L	E	S	A
N	U	R	L	A	F	A	T	I	W
K	N	O	A	M	U	H	I	K	A
Y	N	O	T	E	B	A	P	E	Z
O	P	A	L	S	P	M	U	T	A
A	L	S	U	T	L	A	J	A	Y
R	O	V	E	R	T	Y	A	M	I
J	U	S	T	A	M	A	R	U	M

Taking care of your flute

Although complicated to make, a flute is easy to look after. Remember these rules:

1. When assembling the instrument, avoid grasping any moving parts because you can so easily damage them.

2. Make sure the head-joint and body are in line before assembling them with a slight twisting motion, and adjust the foot-joint to a comfortable little-finger position.

3. If a joint is too tight, don't grease it. Try polishing the tenon with a slightly abrasive silver polish for several minutes. If it's still tight, take it to a music shop.

4. Never put the flute down resting on its keywork!

Chinese flute player

5. After use, always put the flute away in its case. This saves accidental damage, slows tarnishing, and avoids tiny particles of dust getting into the mechanism.

6. Make sure the flute is snug in its case, the right way. Closing the lid carelessly damages many flutes!

7. Never eat, drink, or run around before playing. If you do, moisture from your breath will attack the pads and the inside of the flute. Even when playing for just a few minutes, some moisture condenses on the inside of the flute. Remove this before putting the instrument away by using a special absorbent *lint-free* cotton cloth or piece of silk. Don't put the damp cloth back inside the case.

8. If the flute tarnishes, restore the shine with a flute-polishing cloth. Never use silver polish!

9. Treat the keywork with respect.

Clean the inside

Polish the outside

Fact file

1

The word **flute** comes from the Latin verb *flare* which means to flow. Logical isn't it? Words from the same linguistic root are fluid, floating, flying, flutter, flow...

2

Some student flutes have curved head-joints, which makes them more comfortable for younger children to hold and play.

Curved head-joint for younger players

3

Closed-hole flutes have solid keys. However you press them down, they close the hole and make the sound. Open-hole flutes have perforated keys, which may be more difficult for beginners.

4

Most student flutes are made of silver-plated metal such as yellow brass, which is 70% copper and 30% zinc. Why the silver-plating? Not just to make flutes look nicer: It actually gives a more mellow sound. (Nickel-plated flutes may look nicer in the shop because they are shinier, but they are very slippery when held in sweaty fingers.)
Professional players have solid silver flutes with white-gold springs. **James Galway** is known as the

5

A flute is $26^{1}/_{2}$ in. (67 cm) long and weighs 400 – 600 g, depending on what it is made of.

"Man With The Golden Flute" because he plays an instrument made of solid gold! The Irish jig (page 12) and Gossec's *Tambourin* (above) both sound marvelous when played by him. A few orchestral players in Europe prefer the old-fashioned wooden flute because they feel that it makes the right sound to go with the oboes, clarinets and bassoons of the woodwind section, all of which are made of wood. Most piccolo players in American orchestras play wooden piccolos.

Practice or training?

To be any good at athletics or sports, you must be in training. The same applies to playing a wind instrument like the flute. Think of your flute teacher as a coach who explains what the problems are and how to overcome them, but remember that the real work has to be done by you, the player, in your daily training sessions!

> The one who takes care, in practising of every note, will be at the end a good player.
>
> Theobald Boehm.
>
> Munich the 4' of March 1872.

Simple rules for effective music training
1. Keep fit. Running, swimming, cycling, and athletics all help your breath control, which is the basis of making a good sound.
2. Always practice standing up, with the music on a properly adjusted music stand.
3. Wear comfortable, loose clothing.

Only regular training works! Find a time of day that suits you and stick to it. This might be before going to school, when you get home, or before doing homework.

"How long should I practice?"
Beginners usually start with ten minutes a day. In addition, they play for fun whenever they feel like it. An intermediate level student should practice no less than half an hour a day. Very advanced students should practice no less than one hour a day. The key words are **every day**.

Sample half-hour practice schedule
1. One minute of breathing exercises.
2. Four minutes of tone exercises like the one at the top of the page.
3. Five minutes on the current scales and technical exercises plus the basic scales on pages 18 and 19 of this book.
4. Five minutes or more on current studies, repeating some old ones.

By now you have done quite a lot of work, so take a five-minute break and play for fun – a few easy pieces, pieces you know well, favorite tunes (like Greensleeves at the top of the next page.)

5. Finally, spend ten minutes working on the pieces you are currently learning with your teacher.

More important than how long you practice is how regularly you do it. Ten minutes every day is far better than half an hour twice a week. Every day? Well, some people prefer to have two **No Practice** days each week; for example, when sports or homework or family activities make it difficult to find the time. Get into the habit of regular training by placing a check mark on the Honesty Chart for each day you practice. Remember – **good training concentrates on your weak points.**

FLUTE TRAINING HONESTY CHART

	Mon	Tues	Wed	Thurs	Fri	Sat	Sun
Week 1							
Week 2							
Week 3							
Week 4							
Week 5							
Week 6							
Week 7			—TAKE A BREAK!—				
Week 8							
Week 9							
Week 10							
Week 11							
Week 12							
Week 13							

15

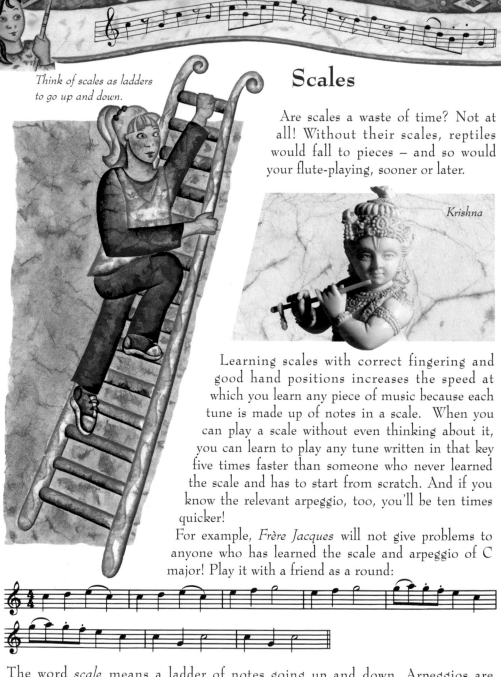

Think of scales as ladders to go up and down.

Scales

Are scales a waste of time? Not at all! Without their scales, reptiles would fall to pieces – and so would your flute-playing, sooner or later.

Krishna

Learning scales with correct fingering and good hand positions increases the speed at which you learn any piece of music because each tune is made up of notes in a scale. When you can play a scale without even thinking about it, you can learn to play any tune written in that key five times faster than someone who never learned the scale and has to start from scratch. And if you know the relevant arpeggio, too, you'll be ten times quicker!

For example, *Frère Jacques* will not give problems to anyone who has learned the scale and arpeggio of C major! Play it with a friend as a round:

The word *scale* means a ladder of notes going up and down. Arpeggios are dangerous ladders because some of the rungs are missing! Notes 2, 6, and 7 are left out, which makes them harder for beginners to learn. Mozart's *Eine Kleine Nachtmusik* (top of page) is based on the arpeggio of C major.

Think of these ladders as the way to climb to the heights of super stardom playing Mozart concertos that include passages like these! (See top of page and below.)

If that seems a long way in the future, remember that scales are required for exams and competitions. There are many kinds of scales and arpeggios, but major and minor are the two basic ones, and the ones you will need the most in your early training.

Practice your scales every day.

'Carnaval de flûtes' by Jennifer Weller

Most easy flute music is based on the scales on the next two pages. Learn them and check off each one each time you play it perfectly.

Two famous pieces of flute music begin with minor arpeggios. If you have learned B minor and G minor, you'll have no problem playing these: the *Badinerie* by Bach (below) and the *Sicilienne* by Fauré (top of next page).

The major scales and arpeggios

Each time you play a scale and arpeggio perfectly, place one tick in the corresponding box.

C Major — ✔

G Major — ✔

F Major — ✔
Bb key on for whole scale

D Major — ✔

Bb Major — ✔
Bb key on   index left off for Eb

When all the boxes are checked, you are ready to play against the clock. Time yourself with a stopwatch or kitchen timer and write in the first box how long it takes to play all five major scales and arpeggios perfectly. The next day, time yourself again. By the end of each week, you should be getting faster and faster.

	MONDAY	TUESDAY	WEDNESDAY	THURSDAY	FRIDAY
Week 1	___min ___sec	___min ___sec	___min ___sec	___min ___sec	___min ___sec
Week 2	___min ___sec	___min ___sec	___min ___sec	___min ___sec	___min ___sec
Week 3	___min ___sec	___min ___sec	___min ___sec	___min ___sec	___min ___sec
Week 4	___min ___sec	___min ___sec	___min ___sec	___min ___sec	___min ___sec
Week 5	___min ___sec	___min ___sec	___min ___sec	___min ___sec	___min ___sec

The harmonic minor scales, arpeggios, and G chromatic scale

Practice these scales and arpeggios. When you have checked all the boxes, play them against the clock.

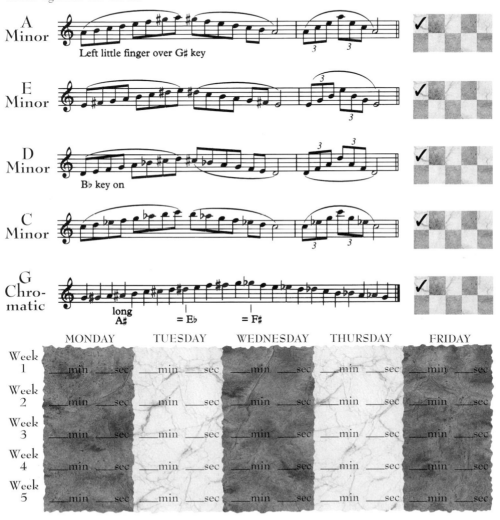

Practicing the chromatic scale may give your fingers a chance with *The Flight of the Bumblebee* by Rimsky Korsakov (see top of page).

Exams and competitions

Examinations

Music exams are a way for every learner to find out just how much progress has been made. Passing an exam tells you and your parents and teacher that you really have achieved the level of knowledge and performance attested by a Grade certificate and are ready to move on to the next stage. Some children find that the idea of a music exam makes them nervous. But in fact the examiners are friendly musicians, all of whom can play one or more instruments. They have all been trained to do the job and understand that the students may be nervous.

Competitions can be fun

In an exam, every candidate who meets the required standard will receive a particular grade and a certificate. Competitions, however, are competitive! To win, you must play better than the opposition. Music competitions are divided into classes by instruments and by age. The judges give marks for accuracy, technique, and musicianship, and the player with the highest score is the winner. Very high-level competitions are judged by panels of up to five adjudicators. The winner may be given a medal, an award of money, a trophy, or a scholarship. At the top competitions, prizes may consist of some paid engagements or appearances on television and radio.

The audience includes the parents and teachers of the competitors and also other people who are on the lookout for talent. Anyone can go just to listen. You can learn a lot, not just from the best players but also from the ones who make mistakes.

You can find out about the competitions you could enter from a teacher or by reading *Flute Talk*, *The Flutist Quarterly*, or *The Flute Network*. Details of competitions and festivals are also available from The National Flute Association and local flute clubs.

Fit to play

Any champion athlete or ice skater will tell you that the secret of giving your best performance is PREPARATION! Poor preparation leads to nervousness on the day, so start your run-up to the big day one month before.

Here are ten tips to get you to peak condition.

1. If you're not fit, get fit! If you are fit, get fitter! Playing the flute needs powerful lungs. Running, yoga, and swimming are good exercise for flute players.

2. Give your flute a check-up. If there is a sticky key or a pad that does not close properly, get it fixed.

3. Practice your pieces in the order you are going to play them.

4. When nervous or excited, we all tend to breathe fast and shallowly. Mark extra breaths in your music. Run up and down stairs, make yourself short of breath, and then play the piece. Wherever you need to breathe, put in a breath mark.

5. Mark the dynamics and check your tonguing.

6. Practice difficult passages slowly. Faults show up at half-speed.

7. Play your pieces through to anyone who will listen.

8. If you have problems with a slurred passage, play it tongued – and vice versa.

9. Write the name of each scale and arpeggio on pieces of paper. Put the papers in a box. Each practice session, pull out six at random and play them.

10. Rehearse your accompanied pieces with a pianist, or ask your teacher to record them for you to work with at home.

Tips for top performance
Before you leave the house

On the day of an exam or a competition, there's a drill to make things easier.

1. DRESS neatly and comfortably. No tight clothing. Comfortable shoes (preferably *not* new). Hair tidy so that it cannot get in the way when playing.

2. You can't play the flute well on an empty stomach, so EAT something even if you don't normally have breakfast.

3. ALL THE FIVES...Take 5 deep breaths. Practice 5 minutes of long notes, then 5 minutes of slow, tongued scales, plus 5 minutes on your pieces.

4. STAMP OUT CHIN-SKID!
   If the skin below your mouth gets moist when you are nervous, the flute will skid away from the lip. Try putting clear nail polish or a  postage stamp on the lip plate, or dabbing some anti-perspirant on your chin.

5. HANDS HOT? When tense, some people have sweaty fingertips which slip off the keys. If this is your problem, dab some anti-perspirant here, too, or use a touch of talcum powder.
   HANDS COLD? If your hands get cold when you are excited, wear gloves just before going into the examination room. Don't be shy. Many professional musicians wear gloves in the dressing room, for this reason.

6. JUST IN CASE... Slip into your flute case the flute-aid kit consisting of an elastic band for a broken spring, some cigarette papers for drying moist pads, and a screwdriver.

7. Pack a DRINK too. You may be kept waiting and get thirsty. (But don't have an ice-cold one just before playing, or you'll lose your embouchure.)

8. Just before you leave the house, DOUBLE-CHECK that you have the address and time of your exam/performance, your flute, your music, and the accompanist's music.

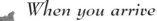

When you arrive

1. Aim to arrive twenty minutes early. This way, if you get caught in a traffic jam, you won't have a last-minute panic.

2. DON'T GET EXCITED by talking too much in the waiting room! The time to chat with friends is afterward.

3. WARM-UP. Like a runner before a race, ignore the other people waiting and have a quiet warm-up for yourself and the flute by playing long notes or a favorite tune.

4. If you still feel NERVOUS, do some deep breathing to calm you down.

5. When you go in, say hello to the examiner or smile at the audience and make sure the accompanist has your pieces.

6. Raise or lower the music stand to the height that suits you.

7. Don't rush the tuning-up. If you need help, ask the accompanist. After warming up in the waiting room, the flute may sound sharp. If so, pull the head-joint out a little.

IN AN EXAM

Don't worry if you cannot finish one of the scales or the sight-reading. As long as you begin and do your best, you will get a grade. If the judge stops you, don't worry; you've probably played enough for a grade.

Candidate's Name
Candidate's Number
Examination center
Time
Instrument

If you make a mistake in one of your pieces, don't stop playing or try to excuse yourself. You won't fail because of this, so just keep playing to the end.

Don't rush the sight-reading! You are allowed to look at it first. If you wish, you can also "ghost it," or play it through once quietly for yourself, before playing it properly to the examiner.

Blowing is not playing the flute; you must make use of your fingers.

JOHANN WOLFGANG VON GOETHE

Mirror, mirror on the wall,
Help me play the best of all...

Perhaps you are not making as much progress as you (or your teacher) would like? Maybe your exam result was not as good as you had hoped? There are 10 common problems, any one of which could be holding you back. These are not beginners' faults; even famous professional players can fall into bad habits. Luckily these problems are easy to detect and easy to cure. All you need is a mirror! It will tell you everything. First take a few steps back so that you can see your whole body. Play a tune from memory and watch yourself. Give yourself a check if the first statement applies to you and an X if it's the second.

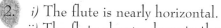

Bad feet and resting arms

Your head, neck, shoulders, and arms should feel as if they are held up by strings!

1. i) Your weight is equally distributed on both feet.
   ii) You are a stork, trying to play with most of your weight on one leg.

2. i) The flute is nearly horizontal.
   ii) The flute plunges down to the right.

3. i) Your spine is straight.
   ii) Your spine is twisted toward one side.

4. i) Your tummy expands visibly when you breathe in.
   ii) You can't see your tummy move when you breathe in.

5. i) When playing, you look yourself in the eye.
   ii) Your head is down so that your eyeballs have to swivel upward to see their own reflection.

24

Now stand close to the mirror and play again, watching yourself, then be honest!

1. *i)* Your embouchure is balanced.
    ii) Your embouchure is twisted to one side.

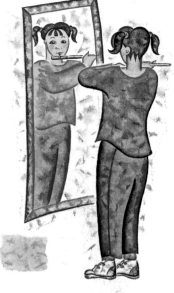

2. *i)* Your lips cover one third of the hole.
    ii) Your lips cover much more or much less.
Covering too much results in a flat and weedy sound.
Covering too little makes a breathy and ugly sound.

3. *i)* Your fingers stay near the keys all the time and are slightly curled so that the pad of each finger always comes down fast and in the right place.
    ii) The fingers not actually on a key are flat and some are nowhere near the keys.
Flat fingers make slow players! Practice trills for five minutes a day looking in the mirror and watch how your finger position improves. Especially get into the habit of keeping the little finger of the left hand over and close to the G# key and make sure that the index finger of the left hand is always off for middle Eb. Practice Eb major scale and Il Était une Bergère (above).

4. *i)* When you breathe in, you keep the flute in position against the lower lip.
    ii) You move the flute when you take a breath.
Moving the flute away from the mouth means that you lose the embouchure and have to fumble for the sound afterward, looking like a goldfish in a bowl.

5. After playing for five minutes, put down the flute.
    i) There is no mark below the bottom lip.
    ii) There is a red mark below your lower lip.
A mark means that you are pressing too hard, with too much tension in your neck, shoulders, and arms. Relax, and hold the flute more lightly.

Little finger sticking up

Le fifre
by Edouard Manet
1866

Fluter, flautist? Pipers all...

What do you call someone who plays a flute? Well, flute player is the safest. Most orchestral players in Britain call themselves flautists because the old name for the flute was "flaute" or "flahute." But James Galway says he's not a flautist because he doesn't play the flaute any more! In the United States, most orchestral players call themselves flutists. Three hundred years ago, Samuel Pepys wrote in his diary, "I saw a fluter playing his flute." Makes sense, doesn't it? Many folk players still use the same word and call themselves fluters.

Ian Anderson, Montreal 1989

It doesn't matter which name we use because, according to Grove's dictionary of music, "The flute is generally regarded as the most perfect of all the wind instruments." But two thousand years ago, the philosopher Aristotle said, "The flute is not an instrument that has a good moral effect because it is too exciting!"

In the nineteenth century somebody else said that the flute was a musical weed that sprang up everywhere. That was probably some jealous oboist or trumpeter.

Marcel Moyse, a famous French flutist, had a different opinion. He called the flute "the queen of instruments."

You can hear Marc Grauwels playing Morceau de Concours *(above) on the CD.*

Flute concert in Sanssouci *by Adolph von Menzel*

In Shakespeare's play *Hamlet*, the prince asks "Will you play upon the pipe?" By this he means the flute. His friend Guildenstern replies, "My Lord, I cannot." "Ah," says Hamlet. "It is as easy as lying: govern these vantages with your fingers and thumb, give a breath with your mouth, and it will discourse most eloquent music."

ROMANCE
From *Eine Kleine Nachtmusik*

Track 6 on the CD is the duet. Track 7 is the second flute part, preceded by metronome count-in of four beats.

W.A. MOZART
(1756-1791)

28

SCARBOROUGH FAIR

On track **10** of the CD this is played on alto flute and piano. You can play it on your flute from the music printed here with the accompaniment on track **11**.

TRADITIONAL

PAPAGENO'S SONG
From *The Magic Flute*

Track 8 on the CD. Piano accompaniment is on track 9.

W.A. MOZART
(1756-1791)

THE ENTERTAINER

Track **16** on the CD. Piano accompaniment is on track **17**.
Watch out for the coda!

SCOTT JOPLIN
(1896-1917)

Moderately

poco rit.

31b

MINUET
From *Suite in B minor*

Track **12** on the CD. Piano accompaniment is on track **13**, preceded by metronome count-in of three beats.

J.S. BACH
(1685-1750)

MINUET
From *Suite in A minor*

Track **14** on the CD. Piano accompaniment is on track **15**, preceded by a metronome count-in of three beats.

G.P. TELEMANN
(1681-1767)

31a

RADETZKY MARCH

On track **18** of the CD this is played on the piccolo.
You can play it on your flute from the music printed here with the piano
accompaniment on track **19**, after the metronome count-in of four beats.

JOHANN
STRAUSS
(the elder)
(1804-1849)

ROCK-A-MY-SOUL
Canon for 2 or 3 flutes

On track 20 of the CD this is played by two flutes. Because this is a round, you can join in with them at the start of any eight-bar phrase.

SPIRITUAL

Treasury of music

Your flute is the key that unlocks a musical treasury for you to enjoy, both by listening and playing. The flute has a colossal repertoire of music written for it. Like a jewelry box with several trays for earrings, necklaces, brooches, and so on, this musical treasure chest is divided into compartments.

Baroque music (1630 - 1730) includes thousands of pieces of music for recorder and the one-keyed Baroque flute. Although these instruments sound quieter than the modern concert flute, orchestras then were so small that the flute and recorder could be heard. From this period come Handel's and Telemann's lovely sonatas. (See Telemann's *Suite in A Minor** at the top of the page). Johann Sebastian Bach wrote many important sonatas. He composed the famous *Suite in B Minor** (which is difficult to play because he forgot that flutists need to breathe!). Listen to James Galway's performance of Vivaldi's concertos *Storm at Sea*, *The Goldfinch,* and *Phantoms* and to Maxence Larrieu's rendering of sonatas by Blavet, Loeillet, and Leclair. If you prefer chamber music, listen to works by Rameau and Couperin. Every flute player knows the name of Quantz, a German Baroque composer who was a flute maker to Frederick the Great and who also wrote more than 300 flute concertos!

Handel

Bach

In **Classical music (1730 - 1830)** symphonic works required bigger orchestras, with two flutes and maybe a piccolo as well. All flutists love Gluck's *Dance of the Blessed Spirits** and Mozart's concertos and flute quartets. Haydn wrote only one flute sonata and Beethoven left one serenade for flute, violin, and viola. Other Classical composers to listen to and play are J.C. and C.P.E. Bach, Reicha, Boccherini, Stamitz, and Danzi. Jean-Pierre Rampal has made wonderful recordings of these composers' works, and you may find some early recordings by Marcel Moyse. Gossec's *Tambourin* makes a successful encore piece with which to end any recital.

Mozart

* *You can hear this on the CD.*   34

During the period of **Romantic music (1830 - 1880)**, orchestras grew bigger and bigger and the flute parts became more and more exciting to play. Listen to Saint-Saens' *Romance for Flute and Orchestra*, Fauré's *Morceau de Concours**, Doppler's *Hungarian Rhapsody,* and Godard's *Waltz*. Kuhlau,

Chopin

Andersen, Boehm, Taffanel, Gaubert, and Popp were all flute players who wrote virtuoso works. Look for recordings by Paula Robison, Jean-Pierre Rampal, and Carol Wincenc. Schubert's *Theme and Variations*, Mercadente's *Concerto,* and Chopin's *Variations on a Theme of Rossini** (above) are often used as competition pieces because they are extremely difficult.

The period **after 1880** is sometimes labeled **Nationalistic music**. French composers wrote a great amount of flute music, which is sheer joy both to play and to hear. Susan Milan has made recordings of works by Koechlin, Roussel, Honegger, Poulenc, Enesco, Milhaud, Debussy, Ravel, Ibert, and Roussel. Camille Chaminade wrote a difficult *Concertino for flute and orchestra* which you will enjoy playing. Marc Grauwels has made some wonderful recordings of this *musique de la belle époque.*

Debussy

Flutists' favorites selected from **Modern** music include sonatas by Hindemith, Henze, Prokofiev, Martinu, Berkeley, and Poulenc, as well as concertos by Arnold, Bloch, Liebermann, Nielsen, Jacob, Martin, and Seiber. Chamber music by Stravinsky and Villa-Lobos is exciting. American composers who have written interesting music for flute include Copland, Burton, Piston, Carter, and Ives. Try to find some of these played by Julius Baker.

Stravinsky

Composers of **Contemporary music**, such as Jolivet, Boulez, Varèse, Messiaen, Berio, Nono, and Dick, have also written for the flute. If you like very modern music, try to hear the recordings of these composers' works by Severino Gazzeloni, Robert Dick, and Andre Valadé. And don't forget Ransom Wilson. Some treasure chest to explore! You'll never get to the end of it...

* You can hear this on the CD.   35

Two flutists from a 14th century manuscript, Escorial, Madrid

Personal repertoire

It is satisfying to fill in and update from time to time your personal repertoire of the music you own, can play, or are studying.

Beginning books (e.g. *A Tune A Day* or *The Foundation of Flute Playing* by Ernest Wagner) _____

_____

Etude books (e.g. Henry Altès) _____
_____
_____

Technique books (e.g. P. Taffanel et Ph. Gaubert)_____
_____
_____

Scale books _____
_____
_____

Examination pieces _____
_____
_____

Books of classical music
_____
_____
_____

Mixed books _____
_____
_____

Unaccompanied solos
_____
_____
_____

Solo tunes with piano accompanist
_____
_____

Flute duets (see duet from the Quantz *Trio Sonata* above) _____
_____
_____

Jazz pieces with piano
_____
_____
_____

Jazz studies _____
_____
_____

Popular music (e.g. *Beatles arrangements, Disney tunes*) _____
_____
_____

Concertos (e.g. *Mozart's D major Concerto*) _____
_____
_____

Other music _____
_____
_____

The magic of the flute

Detail of Magic Flute, *Jennifer Weller*

Poets and composers and artists have always been fascinated by the sound of the flute. Mozart wrote a whole opera about a magic flute, called *Die Zauberflöte.* The story tells how Prince Tamino rescues his girlfriend, Princess Pamina, from the wicked Queen of the Night and the villainous Monostatos with the help of the magic flute, on which he plays the tune above.

The composer Ravel wrote a song called *La Flûte Enchantée,* which is French for "The Magic Flute":

Each note flies from his flute towards my cheek like a mysterious kiss.

Two thousand years ago in Greece, the god Pan was looking after his sheep on the slopes of Mount Olympus when the nymph Syrinx walked past. Pan fancied her, left his sheep, and chased after her. Syrinx was frightened and cried out to her father, who was also a god, to turn her into a reed so that she could hide from Pan. But Pan cut the reed and fashioned a flute from it.

When the French composer Claude Debussy heard this story, he wrote down the tune he thought Pan had played on the flute, called *Syrinx* (below).

The Indian god Krishna was a flute player. One day he was playing a tune (below) in the forest and some girls who were minding cows heard the sound. They forgot all about looking after the animals and ran after Krishna, not knowing who he was. The music was so wonderful that they all wanted to dance. Being a god, Krishna was able to grow enough hands so that each girl could partner him, and he continued playing at the same time!

The Pied Piper could have charmed away the children of Hamelin with a transverse flute. Arnold Bax, an English composer, wrote a mysterious piece of music:

I heard a piper piping,
the blue hills among
and never have I heard so plaintive a song.
It seemed but a part of the hills' melancholy;
no piper living there could ever be jolly.

And still the piper piped, the blue hills among
and all the birds were quiet, to listen to his song.

Joseph Campbell

Playing with others
Making friends with the flute

The flute is a wonderful instrument for making friends because you can play so many different kinds of music on it.

One very strange thing about playing an instrument is that you can have a lot of fun making music that you might not enjoy listening to. So, even if you don't like classical music or jazz, don't let that stop you from joining an orchestra or a jazz band.

Young flute players usually begin playing with others in their school band or orchestra. The best players in school orchestras go on to play in junior and senior county youth orchestras. Very good players make it as far as local or state youth orchestras. These orchestras are modeled on the symphony orchestra and play mainly classical music. In addition, there are chamber orchestras, consisting of violins, violas, and cellos, with a few woodwind and brass players. Chamber music ensembles exist in every possible combination of instruments from one flute and a piano to flute and strings, wind quintets (five players), and wind octets (eight players), not forgetting duos (see both parts of *O Suzannah!* above) and trios.

All serious stuff, so far. But flutes can also play light, popular, and commercial music in concert bands, big bands, wind bands (which have no strings or percussion), jazz bands, folk bands, and rock bands. Ask your flute teacher about local groups and orchestras.

The Musicians *by Master of the Female Half-lengths (c.1490 - c.1540), Hermitage, St. Petersburg*

The National Flute Association Convention

...is fantastic fun. Imagine one hundred, two hundred, maybe a thousand flute players who get together to play in orchestras and groups of all kinds with no other instruments to bother about! There are professional players and celebrities to meet and ask for autographs. Some of these give master classes you can attend. There are performances, competitions, aerobics sessions, even scales classes (would you believe that could be fun?). Specialist flute shops bring along head-joints and alto and bass flutes for everyone to try out, as well as flute music, cassettes, and CDs that may be difficult to obtain in local shops. And everybody spends the whole day thinking about nothing but flutes. This convention is advertised in *Flute Talk, The Flutist Quarterly,* and *Flute Network*.

Summer programs

...are festivals, master classes, and music camps. Some are only for flutes; some offer separate instruction for each instrument and have everyone participating in the orchestral sessions. After a one-week course, your playing should be in another league.

Most courses are residential. Accommodation ranges from luxury to tents. There are swimming and sports facilities, treasure hunts, games, barbecues, and midnight feasts. A terrific way to make new (musical) friends!

Music around the campfire

Do not take up music unless you would rather die than not do so.
NADIA BOULANGER

Becoming a professional musician

"What must I do to become a professional flute player?"

Get real! Imagine that you wanted to be a tennis star or an Olympic athlete. To become a professional musician takes similar ambition, drive, dedication, and perseverance. Do you have it? Are you prepared to sacrifice everything else for your ambition?

Lincoln Center, New York

Get some playing experience! Join every music-making group you possibly can. Learn to play Baroque, Beethoven, and Beatles equally well.

Get in shape! Enter every possible competition. Learn to cope with nerves. Watch and listen to the other players. You have to be better than they are!

Get on the fast track! At specialist music schools, the working day is very long. About half the day is spent on the same sort of classroom subjects as at a normal school. The rest of the time is taken up with flute lessons (twice a week) plus lessons on the piano and probably one other instrument. Then there are lessons on theory and harmony, composition, music history, choir practices, and orchestra and chamber music rehearsals. It's a hard life, but those who are good enough to be accepted and tough enough to last the course have a 50/50 chance of making music their career. Other fast tracks are music scholarships to public schools and pre-college programs at music colleges, where students go out of school hours (usually Saturday mornings) for expert instrumental instruction and a general musical education.

Get nosy! Find out what educational grants or awards you may be entitled to from the school system or charitable trusts to pay for fees and traveling expenses, so that you can go to big-time teachers for extra lessons.

...h music! What a beautiful art! But what a difficult profession!

GEORGES BIZET

Get some practice in!
Talent alone is not enough. One professor of music estimated that it takes 5,000 hours of practice to be good enough to go to a music college. Subtract your age from 18 – the age at which students usually begin at a music college or university – and divide the result into 5,000 hours. That's how much work you must do each year, as well as schoolwork.

Get pushy!
Go to flute days and holiday courses and ask teachers and performers there to give you individual lessons. Attend every live concert you can and ask the orchestral players for consultation lessons. You can't be shy if you want to be a performer.

Take your SATs or ACTs!
They are important when it comes to applying to a music college or university.

Get a picc!
Sometimes there may be too many flute players competing for places in an orchestra. If you can play the piccolo, you double your chances of getting in.

Get doubling!
"Doubling" in music means having a second or third instrument – so keep playing that recorder! The saxophone may look very different but it has the same fingering, so it is easy for any flute player to learn fast.

And – get lucky! All honest musicians will tell you that luck is important. By "luck," they mean what happens to players who have done all the above things.

If that sounds like hard work, it is. But that's the kind of effort it takes to make it in music as a career.

A REAL PRO

Name: Atarah Ben-Tovim

First performance: At school, age 11. Decided at this point to become an orchestral flute player.

Exams: Passed all with distinction (the top mark), between the ages of 11 and 13.

Important year: At 15 passed ARCM, was selected for National Youth Orchestra, played at the Albert Hall under Sir Malcolm Sargent, played a Quantz concerto on TV with the Royal Philharmonic.

Musical studies: Junior Exhibitioner at Royal Academy with Norman Knight, later with Gareth Morris, also at the Academy, and in Paris with Ferdinand Caratgé.

First jobs: Age 21, solo flute with the Sadlers Wells Opera and, at 22, principal flute with the Royal Liverpool Philharmonic.

What next?

Is it easy to get into a conservatory?

No, it is very competitive. Probably only one in 20 applicants will get a place.

Should I audition at a college?

Many universities and colleges offer a wide variety of music degree courses, which would include flute lessons.

What other courses might I do?

Performing arts, media studies, communications, arts administration, music technology, education, music therapy. A knowledge of business studies, law, accounting, languages, and word processing could all be of use to a career in music.

What careers are there for players?

Symphony, opera, and ballet orchestras usually have three or four flutes on the payroll. There are many noncontract orchestras, both symphony and chamber, or for musicals, that use freelance musicians for one or several engagements. The recording industry, broadcasting, film, and TV also use freelance musicians. A very few lucky and gifted musicians will tour the world as soloists or with a chamber group (playing solos such as Mozart's *Rondo* or Poulenc's *Sonata* at the top of pages 44 and 45).

The jazz and rock scene is limited for professional flute players, and folk and traditional musicians make a limited living. Military bands also provide a good job source for young musicians.

C	A	R	T	E	T	T	R	E	V
S	O	L	E	G	E	R	R	O	K
A	L	P	L	J	F	L	E	S	A
N	U	R	L	A	F	A	T	I	W
K	N	O	A	M	U	H	I	K	A
Y	N	O	T	E	B	A	P	E	Z
O	P	A	L	S	P	M	U	T	A
A	L	S	U	T	L	A	J	A	Y
R	O	V	E	R	T	Y	A	M	I
J	U	S	T	A	M	A	R	U	M

Answers to the Word-search from page 11

44

I suppose I'll have to teach?

Teaching the flute, whether in the school system or privately, in groups or individually, can be very satisfying. You can teach privately at any stage of your life and work from home. Music staff in a school can become involved in running orchestras, bands, and choirs, and in arranging, composing, and conducting. If you don't want to work with children you might teach advanced students, work in teacher-training, or run a music center. Other branches of education include administration and inspection, examining, and adjudicating. Music therapy and music and emotional counseling are also both very rewarding jobs.

I don't want to play but I'd like to work with musicians

Orchestras employ an enormous staff, from the general manager to stage managers and roadies as well as tour fixers, education officers, promotion and marketing managers, secretaries, music librarians, program sellers, etc. International festival organizers need to speak several languages.
Concert agencies find work for players, whether they are classical musicians or nightclub singers. They also promote concerts, organize tours, and so on.

What about the recording industry and broadcasting?

There are thousands of different jobs, from secretary to producer, sound engineer to studio manager, film editors, sound editors, technical and lighting engineers, disc jockeys, presenters, and script writers.

Photographs taken during the recording session for the CD

What about commercial work?

There are jobs in music, flute, and record shops, selling, buying, and giving advice. You might make and repair flutes. All musical organizations need people with business skills!

QUIZ

Commercials quiz

Here are 8 tunes from the classical repertoire, all of which have been used in commercials. These are from the original orchestral flute parts.

Clues:

1. French dance

1. Answer:

2. Western

2. Answer:

3. Not evening

3. Answer:

4. Brides hear this

4. Answer:

5. Spanish dance

5. Answer:

6. Tenors sing this

6. Answer:

7. Useful at Xmas

7. Answer:

8. Something blue

8. Answer:

ANSWERS

1. *Can Can* (Offenbach: *Orpheus in the Underworld*)   2. *William Tell* Overture (Rossini)   3. *Morning* (Grieg: *Peer Gynt Suite*)
4. *Wedding March* (Mendelssohn: *A Midsummer Night's Dream*)   5. *Habanera* (Bizet: *Carmen*)   6. *La Donna è Mobile*
(Verdi: *Rigoletto*)   7. *Dance of the Reed-flutes* (Tchaikovsky: *Nutcracker Suite*)   8. *The Blue Danube Waltz* (J. Strauss)

46

ll one's life is a music, if one touches the notes rightly, and in time.
JOHN RUSKIN

Useful information

Flute shops

Flute World (Specializing in flute music and instruments)
P.O. Box 25048, Franklin, MI 48025
29920 Orchard Lake Rd., Farmington Hills, MI 48334
(810) 855-0410; (810) 855-2525

Music orders

Carl Fischer, Inc. *(312) 427-6652; (617) 426-0740*
Frankly Music *(219) 925-2330*
Joseph Patelson Music House Ltd.
(212) 757-5587
Schirmer Music *(212) 541-6236*

Flute societies

The National Flute Association, Inc.
*P.O. Box 800597, Santa Clarita, CA
91380-0597*

Magazines

The Flutist Quarterly (The Magazine of
the National Flute Association)
P.O. Box 800597, Santa Clarita, CA 91380-0597
Flute Talk *200 Northfield Rd., Northfield, IL 60093*
The Flute Network
P.O. Box 9472, San Bernardino, CA 92427

Colleges

Boston Conservatory *Boston, MA*
Curtis Institute of Music *Philadelphia, PA*
Eastman School of Music *Rochester, NY*
Julliard School *New York, NY*
New England Conservatory of Music *Boston, MA*
Oberlin College *Oberlin, OH*

Index

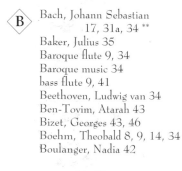